Interview Hacks!

How to Ace Any Interview
for Any Job
at Any Time!

By

David Peters

Disclaimer

This publication is designed to be a resource only and is not meant to be a guarantee of getting a job or offer of employment. Every person is different and every situation is different as well. Because of this there is no one universal approach to interviews or employment. Therefore it is up to the reader to determine the suitability of any or all parts of this book and how they pertain to their own specific situation. The writers, publishers, distributors and resellers of this publication assume no responsibility for the use or application of any or all parts of this book.

Contents

Introduction

Looking for a new or different job can be a stressful process. Since much of that process is controlled and designed by others, there naturally is an element of uncertainty and perhaps a bit of fear involved as well. That is normal and to be expected. In fact, it might interest you to know that the entire process is set up that way for a reason.

While resumes allow companies and people to get a rough idea of who you are and learn about your education and experience, the interview is where they really get to see, hear and interact with YOU. Not the candidate but YOU. Because of there is so much riding on this interview, most people become guarded and afraid and therefore do not do very well.

That is exactly what this book is going to try to help you avoid.

"Interview Hacks" is going to do its best to explain the entire process, what it involves, why things happen like they do and how to do your very best so you leave the interview having made the best possible impression with the people who interviewed you.

If you read this book all the way through there will be very little you don't understand and also very little that will surprise or blindside you. You will have the answers you need to answer the tricky questions they will ask and even more important, you will learn why they ask specific questions and how to craft the very best answers.

All of this is done with one goal in mind. That is to get you through the interview process and come out at the other end with a job offer in hand. That is how we judge whether or not we are successful in the process. It is not how relaxed we were or how we ace a few questions or how dynamite our resume looked. The entire resume and interview process is a results oriented process. That means you are successful if you get the job. Coming in second or third might be nice but it doesn't get you the job.

I would like to set the tone here by sharing with you one very important fact. You MUST understand what I am going to tell you here or you will not do your best throughout the process. It is a simple concept but even though it is simple, some people struggle with accepting it. They struggle because they cannot easily see themselves in a certain way.

What I want you all to start thinking about right now, before we get started, is that this entire process, from resume design through interviews and follow-ups, is a sales process. A sales process with you being the product. While you are not "selling yourself" in a literal way, you are trying to convince others that you are the best "product" out of all the other products out there.

That is a very simple yet effective way of explaining the process. When you look at it this way you become empowered. You see the entire process for what it really is and you understand the need to do certain things and the importance of doing them in a certain way. For most of us, once we get over being called a "product" the rest is easy.

As we go through the book you will find a LOT of information. Some of it will directly resonate with you and your situation while other parts might not. But every part of this book serves a purpose and has a function. Even if you don't think something has value to it read it anyway and attempt to understand it. You never know when that topic or situation might arise in some form during an interview.

I will close by sharing one more important fact with you.

This entire process, like so many other things in life, is often one by doing the little things that by themselves might not have a huge impact but when combined with others can make a huge different. Don't skip over something because it sounds silly or not that important. Because someone else might do it and that might mean that they get an interview or a job and you don't.

Read through the book, take a lot of notes and try to take the materials and make it relevant to you and your situation. When you do that the content becomes a lot more "real" and it will help you discover more about yourself. Your strengths and weaknesses and your good points and bad. Both are equally important because when you know you are weak about something you can turn that weakness into a strength.

Let's get on with help you aces those interviews!

Attitudes & Mindset

In order to set ourselves up for the best possible success, we need to adopt the proper mindsets and understand where we are, where we want to go and how we are going to get there. Just like going on a cross country trip, you would start off without a map or in these days, a GPS! You are going to draw your own map and this book is going to be your GPS.

Below we are going to list a few different subjects pertain to the employment process. Most of this content you already know but our intention is not to show you anything earth shattering new but instead to get you to look at them in an entirely different manner. Because when we look at things differently, we often understand them more and change our behavior towards them.

With that in mind here are 4 things you need to examine before we get started:

It's a Competition – Never Forget That!

Most people think of the employment and interview process as an evaluation process. By that I mean people think that applicants send in their resumes and companies look at them to see if they have the qualifications and education to do the job. If they have what the company requires, they are asked in for an interview.

If that's how you look at the process, then you are wrong and you probably are limiting yourself in your resume and during interviews. Here is how you can correct all of this quickly and easily. You just have to change the way you look at the process.

This entire process is a competition. What the company wants or demands from you is the BARE MINIMUM that you need to have to even be considered. The bare minimum does not guarantee you an interview! It just gets you considered!

Your resume and performance at interviews is going to be measured against other applicants with qualifications similar to yours. Some might be better and others might be worse. But the people who get into the interview phase are thought of as the best overall performers. That means your resume impressed certain people more than other resumes did.

You might not be the best candidate but your resume portrayed you to be. You might not have the best education or experience but your performance at the interview convinced someone you were the right one for the job.

This is all a competition and you are completing against everyone who sent in a resume or responded to an on-line job posting.

This is an important viewpoint because when we look at anything as a competition we soon begin to find ways to give ourselves an unfair advantage. Just like athletes make subtle changes to gain an extra tenth of a second or run a bit faster to outrun their opponents, you will soon be looking for any advantage you can think of to make yourself look better and more impressive in the eyes of others.

Imagine your resume out on a table with 20 other resumes and the top6 get chosen for an interview. Picture interviewers getting together at the end of the day to compare notes on the applicants they interviewed that day. 10 people might have been interviewed with the top 4 going on for a second interview.

Will you be one of those ones who get chosen for the interview or go on for the second interview? Will you be the one who recognized that this is a competition and that every applicants is doing their very best to make themselves look as good as they possibly can. Are you the person who does everything they can possibly do so they get the opportunities others fall short of?

Think of this entire process as a competition where the one who comes out on top gets the job. Not the one with the best education or the most experience. But the one who beats out everyone else and convinces people that they, not anyone else, represents the best fit for the position.

Once you do that, your mindset towards a lot of little things will change dramatically.

Yourself as the Product

This is where a lot of people might have a problem. For many people thinking of themselves as products is despicable. Equating themselves to a box of laundry detergent or a pair of slacks is not something they feel comfortable with. But when you really look at it, that description is very accurate when applied to the employment process.

Think about it for a minute. The consumer (the company that is hiring) is looking for something to solve a problem (doing a job or providing knowledge or skills). So the person they are going to hire is the product that will provide that knowledge, skill sets or other value. IN that sense the person being hired can be thought or as a product.

Now let's turn it around a little bit differently and look at it from the applicant's point of view. IN this view you have many "products" being considered to solve a specific problem.

Just like going to the store to figure out which brand or model will best suit your needs, the resume and interview process is where all the applicants "products" are being evaluated to see which one will be purchased (hired).

Once you understand this and can think of yourself in that manner, your thought process changes as you create your resume and prepare and perform at interviews. It is all about making you appear to be the best product for the job. Once you can feel comfortable with that, you are home free.

Your Personal Sales Pitch

Now that you can think of yourself as a product, let's take a look at how you are going to market yourself to various companies. This involves creating your personal "sales pitch" that you will present to people at the company that you are going to interview with. This is how people will see and interact with you.

Think of your resume as an advertisement with you as the product. Your education and experience become features and benefits. Your resume shows people how effective you are in accomplishing the needed goals of the position. In other words, your resume is an advertisement that ties you into solving a specific problem for the company.

The more problems your resume addresses and potentially solves, the more valuable you look as an applicant.

The interview is your personal "infomercial" where you get to show others how good you are in person or on camera. Your interview takes the words and print on your resume and brings them to life. Your interview is where people get to see and get acquainted with the product and to see and learn things they can't see in a resume.

It is important to realize that everything you do from the initial application to the last interview is one long and detailed sales pitch with you as the product. This might sound a bit crude or crass but it is a very accurate way of looking at the process. Once we look at it in this manner we see the need and advantage of crafting our sales pitch in a very specific and targeted way.

Many others are doing this for their candidacy, shouldn't you be doing it as well?

Getting to the Interview

Last, but certainly not least, there is one more attitude that we must change if we are to be at our most successful selves. That attitude is that most of the work goes into the resume to get us selected and once that is accomplished, the rest is a piece of cake. We need to get rid of that mindset right away.

Yes, the resumes should be designed with its sole purpose to make you appear to be the perfect candidate for the position you are applying for. Every line item should be worded with that intent in mind. Every bit of research should help you identify the right content and the right phrasing. But this is just step one in the process.

Once the resume has worked its magic and resulted in a call or letter stating that you have been selected for an interview, the net phase of work and preparation takes effect. This is where you have to take things to the next level and make sure you are ready for the interview.

Consider the interview as a live resume or sorts. This is where you get talk about what is in your resume and draw the parallels and make the connections between what the company wants and what you have to offer. This is where you get to convince someone in real time.

But there are a few differences and these differences both point to an even greater need for research and preparation. Here are two of the most important ones:

An Interview is Longer

If you were to read your resume all the way through it would probably take less than 5 minutes. But let's say it did take 5 or even 10 minutes for someone to read everything that was in your resume.

An interview might be 30 minutes long or possibly longer depending on the job you are applying for. That means there will be a lot more information being discussed during your interview than there was on your resume.

All of that information is going to come from the questions are going to be asked. Questions that are going to require knowledge and thought and some careful research and preparation. So don't think that just knowing your resume and being prepared to discuss what is in it will get you through the interview. That information is important but it is a fraction of what you will be asked in the interview.

An Interview is Live!

When you created your resume you crated a rough draft and then refined it, changed things around, changed the wording or phrasing and did a lot of other things to make your final copy much, much better and more effective than that original draft. You had time, you had privacy and you were able to think and re-evaluate things as you went along.

Your interview, however, is going to believe. You are going to sit in front of someone, or some people, and you are going to have to think on your feet and come up with answers, good answers, right then and there. You are not going to be able to say something, realize you could have said it better and then take it back and say it again.

You are performing live, with no tape delay and, as circus performers might say, without a net.

So if your plan is to walk in with your resume and field questions on the fly and just say what pops into your head, you might want to rethink that approach. Depending on the job you are applying for, you might be going up against seasoned pros who have been coached and educated and prepared for what is coming. If you don't do the same you are not likely to get the best results.

An Interview Can Be Stressful

I am not trying to scare anyone here but interviews are designed to be somewhat stressful. So you need to get exposed to a bit of stress so you know how to deal with it and react. You want to appear calm and controlled on the outside even though your stomach is churning on the inside. All of this comes through preparation and knowing what is likely to come next.

This way you can calm down, think straight and be at your best. Your answers will be clearer, your impression will be stronger and you will get further in the process as well.

It might surprise you that the entire interview process is more mental than anything else.

People who are able to deal with the mental and emotional aspect of the interview often have a huge advantage over those who are scared or intimidated by it. That is why this book is going to help you so much if you give it the chance.

If you will allow your viewpoints to shift a little bit and if you are receptive to looking at some things in different ways you can ace any interview that might come your way. If you know what to expect and how to come up with the right answers to tough questions and when to say the right things at the right time you can go far.

We are now going to get into how to prepare for your interview. In many respects this is the most important part of the process because what is done at that point will shape how you impress and perform from that point on. So pay close attention, even to the little things, and start preparing for the next interview that comes you way.

Because if you ace that one, it could be years before your next one!

You Need Them More Than They Need You!

We need to get one thing understood really early in the process because some people think this is an even process. That the company needs you as much as you need them. They also think that the company should be equally concerned with what's important to you as you are in what is important to them.

To both of those opinions I say HOGWASH! (Which is a nice way of saying CRAP!)

Unless you are a truly unique person with special skills and talents that nobody else has, you are not as special or valuable as you think you might be. This can be hard for some of us to come to terms with. But the reality is that for every job posting there are about 100 applicants. Many of these applicants will meet the overall qualifications for the job you are applying for.

What this means is that if the company doesn't hire you they will hire someone else. That person will probably do a pretty good job and no one is going to lose sleep because you weren't hired.

I'm not saying this to make you feel bad just to give you a sense of reality and to get you to realize that it is up to you to impress them and not the other way around. You have to convince them to hire you. They don't have to beg you to come to work for them. Sometimes this might not be true but the majority of time it is.

What all of this means is that you go through the process at their invitation and mostly at their convenience. While they might bend to accommodate your schedule they pretty much tell you where to be and when. They set the standards and it is up to you to meet them, not the other way around.

This is one of those times when even the most entitled person on the planet needs to understand that the interview process is centered on you impressing other people to choose you for the job and not the other way around. Once you figure this out you will find your attitude changing for the better and you will soon see the reason and merit for doing certain things in order to make yourself look and appear better.

Throughout this book we will be making suggestions of things you can do to make yourself appear to be the better candidate. It is up to you as to whether you do them or not. But always remember it is up to you to meet their standards and not the other way around.

Don't Sell Yourself Short!

One thing many people do is sell themselves short when it comes to applying for jobs or talking about their accomplishments. But the fact is, most people apply for jobs they don't think they can really do and discover once they're in place they do just fine.

Now this doesn't mean you should apply for any job and just learn on the fly. It is one thing to apply for a job managing 100 people when the most people you ever managed was 5 and applying for a job as a brain surgeon while never going to medical school or having any medical training!

A lot of people "fake it until they make it" when taking on new jobs. As long as your comfort level is fairly high and you know how to go about learning the things you need to learn go ahead and go for it. But if you put yourself in a position where what you do can harm someone else or hurt the company, I would advise you to think twice or even three times about taking that job.

In other words, give yourself credit where credit is due and always try to stretch your capabilities and learn something new. Almost everyone is a little nervous when stepping into a new position. But don't let that stop you. Just be prepared to learn a little faster, work a little bit harder and reduce the learning curve before anyone really catches on.

Judging from some of the people I've worked with over the years, you will do just fine!

Overall Preparation

Get Your Resume Updated and Targeted to the Job

The first thing we need to do is make sure we have a highly targeted and updated resume to take with us to the interview. If you haven't done this then stop right now and get your resume up to date and optimized.

Since this is not a book on resume design and creation I am not going to get into it. I suggest you read our book "Resume Hack" for details on how to create a powerful resume. But let it suffice at this point that every line on the resume should point to just one goal. That is making you appear as the most perfect applicant for the job. Everything should be as relevant and impressive as possible.

Even though you submitted your resume to the company at application, you are going to want to bring several copies with you just in case the person or people interviewing you do not have a copy in front of them.

Stranger things have happened and if they ask you for a copy and you don't have one that will start you off on the wrong foot!

There is not one perfect number of resumes to bring with you but I have found that having six copies is almost always enough to get through an interview. You also want a copy for yourself to follow along with so you make sure you give the same resume (especially dates!) that is on the resume.

It is also perfectly fine to update your resume if you have had significant changes since you originally applied for the position. With some companies taking several months to go through applications it is possible that something important about you has changed since you last submitted a resume.

Prepare Well & Relax More

The one very powerful thing about preparation is the mental benefits it carries with it. The more we prepare for something the more confident we become with our knowledge and abilities. They more we practice and learn and become more informed the more confident we become in our ability to answer any question or handle anything that might come our way.

It's just like studying for a test or taking practice exams. If you study hard and know the material inside and out you are not likely to be nervous during the test.

That is because you know that you are well prepared. After all, if you got over a 95 on 5 practice exams chances are that you will do just as well on this one!

It is insecurity that makes us nervous. If we only know parts of something then we will worry about what might happen if we are asked about something we don't know. This will make us act and appear nervous. Since part of the in-person interview involves watching the appearance and mannerisms of the applicants, preparing yourself well and being calm will help you a great deal.

Being able to relax will help you think better and respond more accurately. It will allows your voice to relax as well so there is little or no nervousness in it. It will also help you to answer questions easily and without endless rambling on because you are afraid you didn't say enough in your answer.

Take Notes & Keep Records

As you go through the preparation process, be aware that you will go through a ton of information. Information you might not feel is useful or worth much at the time but might be valuable later on. So when you apply for any job, make a few notes about the research you did at that time. This will give you a starting point on which to base even more research. There is no reason to do anything twice if you don't have to.

If, for some reason, you didn't do any research before you applied and you managed to get an interview out of a non-targeted or specific cover letter, then thank your lucky stars but do your research now!

Also keep track of when you sent the resumes out, who and where you sent them and any other notes that might help you out later. If there was a personal recommendation or contact you used, remind yourself of that as well. Keep a sheet or paper (or more if necessary) for every job. If you get a request for an interview, pull this paper and add to it as necessary.

Good Enough is Not Good Enough

I know a lot of people who go through life looking at something they had done or created and thinking that what they did was "good enough". Now sometimes "good enough" will be good enough but when competing for a job that is certainly not one of those situations.

Good enough might be good enough when you know everything about a situation or application and you know what is needed. But when you are competing for a job you have no idea who your competition is and what they bring to the table. They might be pulling out all the stops while you sit back with your "good enough" approach.

The reality is that your resume and interview performance has to be good enough to get the job. And that definition of "good enough" is nothing short of your very best. So if you think that good enough really is good enough then be prepared to go out on a lot of interviews and submit even more resumes until you find one job where your "good enough" actually is good enough.

Go Out on "Test" Interviews.

My last suggestions is one that takes the most time and effort but could at the same time provide invaluable experience and information for you regarding interview performance. It involves going out on practice interviews.

In a perfect world you would apply for several jobs before the really important ones come along. This way you can go on interviews and see first-hand what they are all about. While you can read about them and prepare yourself for them, nothing is better than doing well on an interview and getting really positive feedback.

Most of us know what our career goals and plans are and have a rough idea where we should be at one time or another. When we know these things we can make sure we are ready for opportunities when they arise. We can apply for jobs we don't think we are ready for just to get an interview and perfect our interview performance and skills.

We can get in front of real life interviewers and see how they work and how interviews are conducted. We can sit down afterwards and review our performance and answers and determine what we did well and what we should change later on. All of this we do with one ultimate goal: To make sure we are prepared as possible for when the largest and most important opportunities come along.

Do yourself a favor and put some serious time and effort into the preparation phase of the interview process. Prepared people do better and go further than those who don't bother to do the things that can sometimes make all the difference. You might not think this is worth the time and effort but trust me, it is.

Before the Interview

Do Your Homework

Look at the preparation the same way as you would study for a test. Because an interview really is a kind of test and the grade you get might determine whether you go further in the process or not.

Find out everything you can about the company. How big they are, where their offices are located, how many people they employ and even who their CEO is. (That's a common interview question!)

But even take it further and research their competition as well. Find out who they compete with in the marketplace and why they are better or worse than the others. This can help you better position yourself and your skills. Do your best to get acquainted with as much of the overall industry as you possibly can.

Write down statistics such as last year's sales, stock prices, industry sales number of employees and other specifics that might be able to be worked into answers to questions to showcase your knowledge about the company and where it stands in the industry.

Understand the Company and its Wants and Needs

Try and determine the needs and wants of the company as well. What is it they wish to accomplish? Are they looking to grow or are they already expanding. What are the main problems with the company? What is the company looking for in its employees? What does the company place a high value on as far as employees are concerned? What does the company need to move forward?

All of this information can be used to determine how to best represent yourself in the interview. It will allow you to determine how to give them more of what they want and how to make them feel that you are the answer to their needs and problems.

Be a Problem Solver

Speaking of problems, every employee exists to address or resolve a problem. Job responsibilities are designed to make sure that certain things happen so certain problems don't occur. Engineers design safe and durable products so those problems do not occur. Sales people make sure products are represented well and properly so they sell very well. Every position is there to address or solve a problem and you need to understand what those problems really are.

During the interview it is up to you to let them know how you can solve particular problems and why you are the best person to solve those problems. You can bring up specific skills, accomplishments and experience that will all help you become very effective at exactly what it is the company needs from you. Though they might not see it that way if hiring you to fill the impression will make those problems go away then you have a good shot at landing the job.

Connecting the Dots

Hopefully in your resumes you helped make direct connections between your education and experience and what the company is looking for from an applicant. If you have already done this, that's great! If not, you need to start doing it now! You must not leave it up to other to make these connections, you must take it upon yourself to make sure they understand all that you bring to the table and how it relates to them!

This is sort of like those "connecting the dots" drawings and puzzles some of us did as kids. You know the ones I'm talking about. The ones where you draw lines between numbers. The more numbers you connect the clearer the picture becomes. This is exactly what you must do regarding your education and accomplishments.

You need to take every qualification and need and then connect it to something you have accomplished or know about. The more direct connections you can make tying your qualifications and achievements to specific things they are looking for the more relevant you will become to them. This is where and how you can separate yourself from the rest of the applicants.

Think about all of this just like creating that line drawing connecting the dots. As you make yourself more relevant you help create a picture in the mind of the interviewer seeing you in the position and doing a great job. Though the person doesn't actually "see" the picture it forms a powerful impression one the less.

The less you leave to chance the more accurately your "story" will be told to the interviewer. The more "dots" you connect the clearer the picture, the greater the message and the less confusion you will have. All of these are very good for you to have in an interview.

Prepare a List of Likely Questions

Interviews are not one way with the interviewer asking you questions and you answering them. Sometimes they will ask you what questions you might have to ask them.

This can be a great way for you to steer the conversation over to something that is one of your stronger areas and away from your weaknesses.

Prepare questions that will easily lead the conversation to something that you are very good at or have several accomplishments with. Or maybe you have specific knowledge about something most other people don't have. You can then ask a question that will lead into that topic. This allows you to get information about yourself to the interviewer without being obvious and without interrupting the flow of the interview.

Having questions prepared also shows that you put some thought in the interview and that you really do have some interest in the job and the company. It shows initiative and it shows commitment. That is one of the reasons interviewers ask if you have any questions. They want to see if you have really looked into this opportunity. Whatever you do, don't just say "No, you have covered everything. I'm good!"

Google Yourself

Not many people think of doing this but it can be a very important and eye-opening thing to do.

As you know, the internet contains a wealth of information about everything and sometimes every one.

These days just about every company will do an internet search under the same of the applicant especially when they get into the latter stages of the process. Doing a search yourself might help you deal with things they might find. It might also make you aware of what you should or should not do in the future as well.

Many of us are not aware that any time we post a comment or a picture or whenever our name appears in any document or post that it becomes searchable by the search engines. So those drunken Spring Break phots back in College? They're there for the world to see! The comments on Face book? Searchable. The rants on those propaganda websites? Searchable. Those comments you made in anger and then instantly regretted? Searchable.

While it might be possible to get these items removed, it is not an easy process. With freedom of speech also comes freedom to do stupid stuff as well. The only think you might try to do is make a lot of positive comments, post a lot of positive articles and just get your name out there as much as possible in a positive manner. This might push some of those regrettable things further back in the rankings and the company might not go back that many pages.

But the best thing is not to post anything like that in the first place.

But whether or not there is anything bad out there it is best to find out about it now so you can address it openly and honestly if asked about it. Whether you are looking for a job or not it is a good practice to check under you name at least once or twice a year. This can alert you to several things like identity theft.

Interview Yourself or Have Someone Interview You

"Mock" interviews or interviews given to you by other people for practice can be a great way to gain experience and refine your answers to certain questions. Chances are someone else will be tougher on you than you would be on yourself so it is a more realistic experience than it would have been doing it yourself.

Pick out all the questions that you feel you are likely to be asked and also give the person interviewing you the ability to throw in a few other ones as well just to keep you on your toes and thinking right.

As far as your role in concerned, try and treat this as an actual interview. That means no stopping to think or stopping in mid answer to go back and start over. You can do multiple interview to help you get more comfortable but as each one is going on, treat it as the real deal.

Tell the person interviewing you to not go easy on you either.

The real interviewer isn't and neither should the practice person. If possible, get someone experienced in either the industry you are applying in or someone with Human Resource experience that knows how real interviews are done.

Practice

As you go through the practice stage, stop yourself and go over anything that you do not feel confident in. Be honest with yourself and don't tell yourself that you did well when you know you didn't. Just keep practicing things until they become second nature to you. Above all, throughout the entire process, be honest with yourself.

Part of the practice experience is identifying weaknesses and turning them into strengths. If you are not honest with yourself that is most certainly not going to happen.

When Should You Start Practicing?

Ideally, you should start practicing long before you actually have an important interview. Confidence takes time to build. Also, giving yourself the time you need will remove a lot of the pressure from the process. It is hard to practice something right when your interview is at noon time tomorrow!

Give yourself plenty of time to do it and do it right. They say practice makes perfect and while we don't need perfect, we do need pretty close to it!

Main Types of Interviews

To make things even more interesting you should be aware that all interviews are not the same. Different people conduct interviews in different ways and there are different types of interviews as well. What this means is that there is no one perfect and universal approach to every interview.

To help you prepare for any interview you might run across, here are some of the most common interview types. The interview you actually go out on will probably be one of these type. Or. It might be a blend of two or more of these types. Either way, once you understand them you can prepare for them and do quite well.

Here are the most popular interview styles / types:

Screening Interviews

These are mostly interviews done over the phone to find out additional information or to see if the person is still interested in the job.

There also might be a bit of confusion about something on the resume or specific questions that need to be answered before the process moves forward to an actual interview.

These are common when applicant live a considerable distance from where the regular interviews take place or to reduce the number of applicants to be considered for the full interviews.

These are very short interviews, generally less than a half hour and sometimes much less. Applicants finding themselves at this point should be encouraged that they have made it this far. This usually means that they have met the minimum qualifications and at least are being considered at this time. While this "pre-interview" does not always lead to a full interview, it is still considered an encouraging sign.

Telephone or Skype Interviews

When applicants come from all over the country, or whenever travel becomes an issue for either the company of the applicants, sometimes telephone interviews are given first to make sure only the most qualified people are flown in for further interviews.

These interviews last longer and are pretty much the same as in-person interviews as far as questions and information exchange. The main difference is that unless the interview is done over Skype or a Webinar platform the interviewer cannot see you and you cannot see the interviewer.

One downside to a telephone interview is that you have no idea how serious the interviewer actually is or whether there is anyone else listening in or in the room with the interviewer. Though they are supposed to inform you, the interview might also be recorded as well.

As with any interview, be careful what you say and how you say it. One advantage to a phone interview is that you can have your notes opened or your computer on and search for information as you need it. This is not a substitute for good preparation but it can help if you are asked something you were not prepared for.

Though there are exceptions telephone interviews usually do not end with an offer of employment. Instead they are just the first interview of two or three. Most of the time applicants that pass the first interview will be brought in for a face-to-face interview or two before any offers are made.

Standard Interview

This is the most common type of interview and therefore the one you are most likely to face, especially for a first interview. This is where the interviewer goes over your resume and asks you a series of questions designed to get you to open up about yourself, your education and experience. If is a free flowing of information mostly initiated by the interviewer.

These are the easiest kinds of interviews to prepare and practice for because you just have to think about answers to the most common interview questions. Once you have those answers committed to memory it is all about appearance, demeanor and impressions.

Standard interviews generally take between 30 minutes to an hour and you might get a little tour of the business is there is time. It is a "get to know you" type of interview that gives the interviewer a chance to see the personality behind the resume. It is also where they get to evaluate your appearance as well to make sure it fits their corporate culture.

Behavioral Interview

These interviews concentrate on behavioral aspect of the applicant and are usually encountered I second or third interviews. This is where they ask you how you would react to certain situations and how you get along with others. They will ask you about your communication skills and other "soft" skills.

These interviews also dive into your values, morals and decision making capabilities as well. Because of this be very careful how you answer these types of questions. They are designed to get you to share information that they might not be allowed to ask you under the law. Answer as honestly as you can while framing your answer in an acceptable manner and keep the answers short and sweet.

Situation Interview

This is where they sit you down and ask you how you would handle certain situations. They ask you what you would do in this situation or how you would handle that situation. These questions are designed not only to test your knowledge but also your decision making skills, your values, your honesty and integrity.

Sometimes these questions might all seem very innocent but they are designed to see how you would react to certain requests, pressures and situations. What you do and how you react often will give them a great deal of knowledge about who you are as a person as well as an applicant.

They are useful because most interviewers realize that most applicants practice the routine questions and have pre-designed or "canned" answers.

But these situational questions are not easily practiced for and reveal more of a true reflection of the applicant.

Case Study Interview

Similar to a situational interview, a case study interview is where they show you something that already happened and ask you what you might have done differently or better in order to get a better result.

These interviews are designed to test several things at once. They are testing your knowledge, your decision making, how well or poorly you can evaluate a situation and you problem solving and interpersonal skills. All in one simple exercise.

The key to performing well in these interviews is being able to process information and uncover all the details. If something appear missing, it might have been left out intentionally to see if you would ask. Evaluate everything, ask questions as needed and rely on your knowledge and expertise to help you arrive at the best possible answer.

Often times there is no one really right answer. The interviewer is less concerned with the answer you gave as they are about how you arrived at that answer. If your deductive skills were good and your reasoning is sound, that is what's important. How you arrived at your decision is what they are really most interested in.

Case study interviews are usually reserved for advanced interviews and not first interviews. A possible exception is when someone well known with a great reputation is brought in to talk with people before being hired. In those case they might dispense with the formalities and get right to the important stuff.

Presentation Interview

Almost always reserved for advanced interviews this is where you are asked to give a presentation on some skill or activity directly relevant to the job you are being considered for. If you applied for a sales position, for example, you might be asked to prepare a PowerPoint presentation on the latest product and present it to a group of people.

This is aimed at looking at how well you speak to others and how well you related to different people. They will see how you react to interruptions and questions and who well you stay on track and on message.

If a specific skill is required they might ask you to demonstrate that skill as well in front of a group of people. If you want to be a teaching you might be asked to present a lesson to the group. If you are applying for a position dealing with customers, they might ask you to do some role playing to demonstrate your approach and soft skills.

These interviews are given to see how you perform and communicate with other people. If you are applying for a position that has high visibility and a lot of communication skills, this might be the type of interview you encounter near the end of the interview process.

Demonstration Interview

This interview is almost the same as a presentation interview except that it is more geared or aimed at demonstrating one's skills. For example, if you wanted to hire a piano player for your club, you would want to hear them play a few songs. If you were looking for graphics artist, you might want to see them create something for your company at the interview.

Demonstration skills are great for people whose skills are top notch. If your skills are the best you can truly shine your way through this interview with little or no effort. But if your skills are not top notch, this interview could very well reveal that to everyone.

So if you are applying for a job requiring specific skill sets, do your best to refine them just in case you are asked to demonstrate them during this type of interview. I\even if it never comes to that your improved skills will help you do a better job once you are hired anyway. So it's a win-win for everyone.

Panel or Group Interview

These are the interviews that strike fear in the hearts of applicants far and wide. This is where you sit or stand in a room and are interviewed by several people at the same time. Sometimes this is one way of having multiple people interview you at the same time saving time in the process. Other times it is just to see how well you perform under more pressure and how you can relate to a group of people rather than just one.

These interviews can be difficult because of the different personalities sitting around the same table. There might be interruptions or several people might be talking at the same time. This could even be done on purpose to see how you react under such chaos.

I have always found that it works best to signal out one or two of the most difficult people as you perceive them and then concentrate on them. The reason being if you can satisfy the most demanding people you stand a good chance of impressing the others as well. It doesn't work the other way around.

This type of interview can really make you shine if you handle it well. But if you are easily intimidated you had better deal with that first as those feelings can get you in trouble fast.

But keep in mind that if they truly are considering you for the job, which they probably are, they will give you a fair shot and are just wondering how well you can control and command the room.

Of all the types of interviews, this is the one where being confident in yourself and your abilities really helps. If you believe in yourself and what you are capable of it won't make a difference whether you are talking to one person or 50. Your confidence will show through and you will do just fine.

Luncheon Interview

While this might seem to be the most comfortable and innocent of interviews, you had better be careful and bring you're a game because it can also be the most dangerous!

Interviewing over lunch or dinner is meant to get you to relax so the interviewer can get closer to the "real you". They want you to lower your "applicant persona" and be more yourself and perhaps share more of you than you really should.

During the meal you will discuss yourself and the company and you will answer pretty much the same questions that you would be asked had you been sitting in an office with the person sitting across the desk from you. That part is pretty straightforward. It is the personal questions or the small talk that can get you in trouble.

Keep the conversation contained to "safe" areas. Safe areas avoid politics, sex, religion, morals, values and other personal areas. Also stay clear of offensive or off-color jokes and inappropriate comments about anything. In other words, talk just like you would if your two grandmothers and your minister were sitting at the table with you.

Order something easy to eat that is not messy or easy to spill. Chances are you will be a bit nervous so stay away from soup. Also stay away from finger food such as ribs which are messy to eat. Have a burger or a sandwich or something safe and easy to eat.

As far as beverages are concerned, NEVER order wine or anything containing any kind of alcohol even if the other person has ordered that and encourages you to do the same. Stick with water, soda or iced tea. After all, you want to keep your head clear and capable of controlling what it is saying and thinking. Alcohol and interviews definitely do NOT mix!

Stress Interview

This is a strange type of interview because it seems like everyone there is looking to make you fail. People might be hostile towards you, argue with you at every opportunity and make you have to work hard to make every point or win any exchange.

You might feel that it is you against everyone else because that is exactly how they want it to be.

In these types of interviews it is important to understand that they really do want you to succeed. But in order to pick someone will succeed in a high pressure or high stress job they need to make reasonably sure the person is capable of handling these high stress or uncomfortable situations when the occur. So instead of trying to determine whether you can or can't deal with them, they create one.

The important thing is to remain calm and in control even though people might be doing their best to frustrate or distract you. Stay on point and stay on message. If necessary stop talking and take a breath and then try to reassert control over the situation. When people interrupt you deal with it calmly and respectfully and do not allow yourself to be distracted. Just tell the people who are interrupting you that you will answer their question once you have finished answering the current question.

If people are rude or use offensive language, do not reduce yourself to their level. Always treat everyone with dignity and respect. If it gets too much, you might want to comment on the language and ask that they refrain from using it. Use your judgment on that one although they might be trying to see how you will respond to poor language.

Sometimes you might think that thing were taken a bit too far or you might be too offended by what had taken place. When you get to that point you might want to ask yourself if these people are just playing roles in the process or if they really are arrogant and offensive jerks. If they are just playing a role that is one thing. But if they really are arrogant and insensitive jerks you might want to re-visit whether or not you really want to work for a company that would employ such people.

Chances are any interview you encountered will be one of these types or at worst a blend of a couple of different types. But now you know what to expect and what is behind each type of interview. You know that questions might not always be what they seem and you know that you should be careful of what you say and why you said it.

If you move forward with the approach that every word you say and every action you take should bring you closer to landing the job, then you should be just fine. Just keep on point and on message and do not allow others to distract you from what you want to accomplish or trick you into saying something you shouldn't.

If you can manage all of that, you will do just fine.

During the Interview

The Basics

Now we are getting ready to get to the interview. We have done our preparations, we have practiced the most common questions and we have done a few practice interviews as well. We know all about the company, their competition and all the other important information we should know and we're all set to go.

So now all we need is to go over a few things that might seem like common sense but still are mistakes many people make because they just weren't thinking or because they just didn't feel it made much of a difference. Whatever the reasons might be, be aware of the following so that you make the best impression you possibly can.

Be On time

You are looking for someone to give you a job. A job where you will be expected to be reliable and show up on time every single day unless you have a good reason for being late.

Don't start off on a negative by not arriving on time for your interview. Unless you have a good reason, and this is communicated to the right people ahead of time, this could throw you right out of the running.

Give yourself extra time and take traffic into consideration as well as the weather. Plan on arriving at least a half hour before your interview. You can always sit in the car and read a book or go for a cup of coffee. But you want to be where you are supposed to be at least 15 minutes early ready and willing to go.

Be Nice

Contrary to what some people think, nice people generally do better than nasty or surly people. People who get along with others are generally preferred over the entitled obnoxious full of themselves type of person.

Personality and demeanor are two things that are very important in an interview. The interviewer is going to want to see that you are skilled enough to do the job and nice enough to fit in well with your co-workers. Come up short in either category and you probably won't get the job.

Look Nice

I realize that appearance is just on the outside and doesn't necessarily speak to the kind of person you are or how skilled a worker you can be. But how you look is a critical part of the first impression people make of you. Most of the time they see you before speaking to you so it is in your best interest to look the way people in that job expect you to look.

If you have a problem with people judging you by your appearance you have every right to feel that way and to look however you want to look. But as we already have said it is up to you to impress them not for them to accept whatever you want them to accept. The decision is your and yours alone.

But if you insist on going to that financial planner interview with 14 facial studs and four nose rings to go along with the purple hair and the 74 tattoos, don't be devastated when you are not chosen for the position. There are choices to be made and we live with the consequences of those choices.

Appropriate attire might be professional attire or business causal depending on the interview and position. Personally I advise men to wear a suit or at least a jacket and tie and women to wear a nice dress. This is regardless of the position you are applying for. Proper attire shows respect for the company and the interviewer as well as a commitment on your part towards the position.

Be Courteous

You should be courteous all through your life but especially to everyone you speak to when you come in for your interview. And by everyone I mean everyone. Some companies will make you wait for a while and then ask the receptionist how you were while you were waiting. Did you sit there patiently or did you complain and stare impatiently. Sometimes every part of the visit from the time you walk in until the time you walk out is watched and scripted for a purpose.

Be Positive

Interviewers LOVE positive people. Spend the interview making nothing but positive statements. Tell them what you can do and what you have done. Don't waste time telling them what you can't do or talking negatively. If they ask you about something negative do your best to turn it into a positive by the end of the answer.

Turn mistakes into learning lessons and hopefully have examples where learning from a mistake helped you do better in the future. Eliminate negative words and phrases and make everything as positive as possible. Almost everyone likes positive people better than negative ones. That includes co-workers as well which is why this matters so much.

Be Confident & Strong

Interviewers love people who are confident in who they are and in their skills and abilities. They want people who are not afraid to make a decision or to speak their mind. They do not want someone so insecure that they won't do a thing unless someone approves it in advance.

The most productive people in this world are the ones who are not afraid to take action quickly when they know what the right thing to do is. Indecision costs time and money and can also result in lost opportunities and customer dissatisfaction.

Keep in mind, though, the while interviewers love confidence and strength, they do not like obnoxious or arrogant people. Do not come off as thinking you are better than anyone else even if you might feel that way. Explain your accomplishments without bragging. Discuss your successes without boasting. Show your strengths with humility and reserve. In other words, let your actions and accomplishments speak for themselves at least some of the time.

Show Passion!

Too many people approach a job opportunity as a way to get a bigger paycheck or an extra week's vacation. But those motivators work for just a short period of time.

Once you become used to the larger paycheck and the extra time off the real problems of the job soon resurface. This is something that recruiters and Human Resource people are well aware of.

What they want to see from their applicants is a passion for the opportunity and the company. They want to see people who have researched the company and know what the job is inside and out. They want to hear ideas the applicants have about how they can help makes things better and help the company grow.

In other words they want people who are thinking about the job first and the paycheck second. Whether or not that is reasonable is debatable but for now let's give them what they want to see and sort out the rest later!

Ok, those are a few of the basics when it comes time for you interview. Now let's switch gears a bit and discuss what attitudes you should have as you walk through the door. Because attitudes have everything to do with presentation and your interview is just one big presentation with you on center stage.

Here are a few things you should consider when it comes to how you react and behave during your interview:

Be a Problem Solver

The job you are being interviewed for exists because of certain needs and certain problems. You need to look at your approach in this interview as being the world's best problem solver. You need to show the interviewer and the company how you are able and capable of solving their problems.

Chances are at some point you will be interviewed by the manager of the department you will be working in. what better way to interview with that person than telling him how hiring you will reduce the problems that make it across his or her desk every day. Imagine the impression you would make as you explain to him how hiring you would make his own job easier and less stressful.

Can you think of a better way to get someone to hire you? I can't.

Think Like the Hiring Manager

Much along the same lines, know who is interviewing you and their position in the company. Usually they will give you that information in their introduction. Then address every answer to every question in the way someone in that position wants to hear it. Make the answers as personally relevant as they possibly can be.

If you are interviewing with your future department head, answer each question with how what you would do would make their department better, more productive and higher functioning. Make them aware that a better operating department would mean less stress for the manager.

Talk about every one of your skills and accomplishment in ways that make it obvious as to how they would benefit their department and the company. No generic statements but instead highly targeted and pointed statements designed to impress the interviewer in his or her role in the company.

Answering Questions

While being relaxed can be a huge advantage during an interview it can also cause you problems as well. Be on guard as you answer questions trying to answer each one as completely as possible without saying too much at the same time. In other words, give them full and complete answers to every question and then stop talking. No small talk and no personal stories except for be sociable and nice to the interviewer.

A lot of interviewers will ask you questions designed to get you to talk and volunteer information you otherwise would keep to yourself. Be relaxed but be guarded and careful at the same time.

That is another reason why practicing answers to the most common questions will help you answer questions without providing too much extra information.

Stay on Message

If you have done your homeowner you probably will have a message and a game plan in mind when you sit down for the interview. Try to stick with that plan and approach and do not give mixed or conflicting signals. Unless you see that your original approach is clearly not working, stay on point and try to return the conversation back to where it was previously going.

If you start out with one focus and change it in mid-stream the interviewer is going to wonder if you are sincere or just telling them what you think they want to hear. You want to stay on point, establish your credibility and keep your message and your focus intact throughout the entire interview.

Limit Small Talk

You want to remain friendly but watch small talk at the same time. A skilled and experienced interviewer will know how to steer the conversation around to get you to release personal information or information that you otherwise might have kept to yourself. Keep small talk to a minimum but remain friendly and engaging at the same time.

As we have already said, stay away from politics, religion and other polarizing subjects as well as off color or ethnic humor. Sometimes what you say and what you talk about can provide a real insight into who you really are. Think twice before you speak and if there are any doubts, don't say it. It is better to be safe than uncertain.

Common Interview Questions

Questions asked in interviews are not always what they might seem. Most questions are open-ended questions which means that they can usually not be answered with just a yes or a no answer. These questions are designed to get you to talk.

The interviewer wants you to talk so they can learn something about you that maybe they are not allowed to ask you. They hope you will share certain insights into your personal life and your morals or values as well. The more you talk the more likely you are to say something perhaps you shouldn't have said.

With that in mind it is a good policy to answer the question you are asked with a complete answer and leave it at that. Do not go off on tangents or tell funny stories or relax too much. Because that is when little bits of information and knowledge about you can slip out and hurt your chances for getting the job.

Hear the question, think about the answer and give it. Then wait for the next question. Don't say more than you have to but do not give one or two word answers either.

Here are some of the most common interview questions, why they are asked and how you might go about answering them. Remember that the questions all will pertain to a specific job so you might have to answer them a little differently than the examples below. Just think before you answer about why they are asking the question in the first place and then craft your perfect answer.

Here are some popular interview questions:

What are Your Strengths?

Be honest and do not be afraid to brag a bit if you have accomplished some impressive things. But do not be obnoxious about it or go over the top. Tell them your accomplishments, why they were important to you and what they meant to the company. Remember if you don't let them know, they never happened as far as the employer is concerned.

What are Your Weaknesses?

Everyone has them so don't say you don't have any.

Instead, prior to the interview think of a coupe or weaknesses you had at one time and how you turned those weaknesses into strengths. That is what employers want to see and why they ask this question. If you say you don't have weaknesses, they will know you are lying!

Why Are You Interested in Working for Us?

They want to know that you are not just looking for a paycheck from anywhere but instead for specific reasons why you applied there and not somewhere else. Your research into the company should give you some information that will allow you to come up with an answer that shows you know something about the company and know why it would be a good fit for you.

Where Do You See Yourself in 5 Years? 10 Years?

This question is designed to gauge your sense of commitment. While no one really knows where they will be in 5 years let alone 10, they do not want someone who sees themselves as CEO in 5 years or some other outrageous expectation. Instead, they want to hear about your intended advancement plan and how it might fit into their company structure.

Why Do You Want to Work For Us?

This is one of the most important questions you are likely to be asked.

Employers want to see a mutual benefit for both the company and the employee. They want to see how the candidate feels about the company and how they see them growing with the company. If the candidate has no idea what the company is all about and why it would be a good fit, the interview might be all over at that point. Work on this one carefully before the interview.

Why is there a Gap in Your Employment?

Gaps in employment are red flags because it shows something happened that kept you out of work for a period of time. It is best that they never discover this and there are things you can do with your resume to hide small gaps. But if they are aware of a gap or two, explain it to the best of your ability and try to put a positive spin on it whenever possible. Stuff happens in life and it is how we react to those situations that matters more than the situation itself sometimes.

What Accomplishment are You Most Proud of?

This is where you get a chance to tell the interviewer about something good that you accomplished and why it was so important to you at the time. If you have a great story about a victory or accomplishment that you are really proud of, now is the time to let everyone know about it. But again, be proud but not obnoxious.

Tell Us About a Mistake You Made & How You Recovered From It.

Everyone makes mistakes so don't tell anyone you never made a mistake. Instead tell them about something you did wrong, how you recovered from it and what you learned from the experience so it never will happen again. This is where you show strength and the ability to recover when things don't go right. It is an important skill to have in the business world.

What Can You Offer that No One Else Can?

This is where you launch into your 60 second infomercial on what is special about you and what only you can bring to the table. Be strong and confident but not obnoxious. They are looking for someone special not an egotistical jerk.

Tell Us How You Handled a Problem with a Co-Worker or Staff Member.

Everyone has had problems with some of the people they have worked with so don't say you always get along with everyone. Instead you can say that you are easy to get along with and have excellent "people skills" that allow you to see both sides of something and act accordingly. Then give them an example of a tense situation and how you resolved it using your skills.

Why Should we Hire You?

This is where you show the connection between your skills and the needs of the company. This is where your research and homework really pays off as you can give relevant examples of your skills and knowledge and how the company will benefit from both. This is where you "connect the dots" for the interviewers.

Why Are You Looking to change Jobs?

This can be a tricky one at times depending on the real answer. They want to see if you are looking for more money which can give them the impression that you will be gone when something better comes along. What they are looking for are people who want to improve their position and career, get new challenges and position themselves for better opportunities.

If you were fired, tell them why without being negative and explain how you have changed since then and why it made you a better person. If you quit because you hated your boss, don't tell them that just say that you valued the experience but it had become time to move on and leave it at that.

Tell Us About Our Competition.

This question is just to see if you bothered to take the time to research the company prior to the interview.

Companies want people who are passionate about where they work and only want to work in companies that are a good fit. If you applied without knowing anything about the company that does not look good for you. Do your research so you can answer this question.

How Do You Handle Pressure?

Some people react to stress by crying and huddling in a ball. Others meet stress head on and kick its butt. Most of us are somewhere in the middle of those two extremes. Let people know you deal with stress through a lot of preparation and skill and constant learning. Let them know you learn from your mistakes and that knowledge has just made you stronger not weaker. Don't tell anyone you have no stress because everyone has stress in their life.

What Was Your Biggest Failure?

This is how the interviewer finds out how you react to failure. Do you make yourself stronger? Do you learn from your failure or do you blame someone else. Companies are looking for people who take responsibility for their actions and learn from both their failures and successes.

What Motivates You?

Here is where they hope to get a little bit of insight into who you are and what drives you.

They want to know if it is money or power or status or something else that drives you. From your answer they will decide if they think you will fit in with their corporate environment. Tell them that accomplishments and growth motivates you to do well in both individual and team environments.

What is the Name of Our CEO?

Again, here is where your research will either pay off or expose you as lazy. Just do the damned research, OK?

What Does Your Current Boss Say You Should Improve On?

Pick a few minor weaknesses that you used to have and what you did to turn them into strengths. Then, so you don't give them the impression that you think you are perfect, mention one or two really minor weaknesses you have now and how you are currently turning those into strengths as well.

How Would You Fire Someone?

This is where you can show them that you have compassion but still realize what has to be done and are not afraid to do it.

This is where you can also show your knowledge of various labor and Human Resource policies and mention the required steps that usually need to be taken before someone can be fired. If you are interviewing for a management position, this question might come up.

Are You a Leader or a Follower?

This is a tricky question because good workers are sometimes leaders and at other times followers. No one can lead all the time as no one has all the knowledge all of the time on every subject. I just say that in areas where I feel strong I step up and assume a leadership role. But in situations where someone else is stronger or more qualified I accept a follower role for the good of the team or company. It's hard to argue with that answer.

What Would Your Direct Reports Say About You?

This is where you are asked to evaluate yourself through the eyes of others. They want to hear that you were well respected and were also a hard worker. They want to hear that you are willing to sacrifice personal gain for the sake of the team or company and that you were dependable and honest. They also want to hear that you have values and are known to do the right thing regardless of pressure or consequences. So formulate a few of these traits into you answer.

For most of these questions there is no one perfect or right answer. Instead the interviewer is looking for what you are thinking and how you arrived at a particular answer. So just having the right answer is often not enough. You should be able to explain how you came up with that answer and why. So don't have someone create answers to the questions and just memorize them. If you don't know what the answer means, you shouldn't say it. If someone does create or write answers for you, ask them to sit down and explain all the answers so you can explain them to the interviewer.

Inappropriate Questions

There are some questions that interviewers are not allowed to ask by law and others that just violate personal boundaries and common sense. When you encounter these questions you have a sometimes tricky decision to make. You can refuse to answer these questions which is your right. But the interviewer might take offense and disqualify you from further consideration and site any number of other reasons so you cannot sue them for discrimination or anything like that. Violating the law is one thing, proving it played a role in the hiring process is something else entirely.

You can choose to answer the questions which you should be careful about since sometimes the question might not be what it seems to be. Or you, if the reason behind the question is obvious you can answer the question by not really answering it specifically.

For example, one question you are not allowed to be asked is your age. That is because you cannot discriminate against someone based on their age. So you cannot deny someone employment because they are 60 years old or any other age.

If you are 60 and someone asks you your age, you might answer something like this. "I know that is something you shouldn't be asking me but I can see where that might be a concern of yours. So let me address that. I have a lot of years left in me that I plan to work and my experience gives me an advantage over people much younger than I am. Plus, I have a work ethic that is second to none. So if you have any concerns about my age, let me assure you they are completely unfounded."

You just answered his question and addressed his concerns without actually telling him how old you are. In this answer you made him aware you knew it was an illegal question but you answered it with dignity and respect and treated the interviewer in the same manner. Remember, you have to impress the interviewer and not the other way around.

Interviewing the Interviewer

During every interview there comes a time where you are allowed to ask a question, provide additional information or lead the conversation down a specific path of your choosing. You should never let these opportunities pass you by. You should always be thinking at least one or two steps ahead. So as this interview winds its way down you need to make your final appeal for further consideration and learn a few things that might help you further down the road.

Here are a few things to consider when asking questions of the interviewer and getting additional information out in the open that might have otherwise gone unnoticed.

Interview Handouts & Other Information

We discuss this in more detail in "Resume Hacks" but sometimes there is just not enough room in a resume for all the education, experience and accomplishments you might have to offer.

So to make sure all or any of that extra information is not lost in the shuffle, you can create "fact sheets" that include any relevant information and bring them along with you and present them to the interviewer.

I like to wait until we are discussing my accomplishments and experience and then I present them with the fact sheet saying to the interviewer "Her are some more of my accomplishments and background that you might find helpful." The result is the interviewer not only can look at the information now but it will likely be included in the information folder about me when it moves up the line to someone else.

Just make sure that whatever you give the interview has distinct relevant information pertaining to the job you are interviewing for. Do not bore them with unrelated details or how which scoring records you set while in High School. Only relevant information should be included.

Salary & Benefit Issues

Money usually does not come up in the first interviews unless the subject is raised by the interviewer. Do not bring it up yourself as this is not the place or time. The only exception might be if the next step in the process involves considerable travel or commitment and you would not want to invest that in a job that paid far less than you expected.

But even then, you can raise that topic when you know you are going to the next step.

Benefits are another issue as they are usually gone over quickly during the interview as a way of giving you a bit of information pertaining to the company. They are not gone into in-depth but are presented at an overview level.

As you go further into the process meaning a second or third interview, then benefits and salary become part of the process and are negotiated between the company and the applicant. If the job is being decided on the first interview discussions might be held then or be done over the telephone as the offer is made.

Your Questions for the Interviewer

You will usually be asked if you have any questions and you can use this opportunity to address any points you thought might not have gone as well as you hoped or if you had thought of anything new as the interview progressed. Questions can help in the transition between topics you wish to expand on.

For example, you might ask if the interviewer had any specific concerns about your background or abilities. This can be useful in two ways.

If you are moving ahead in the process you can take the time to address those concerns and possibly turn a concern into a strength. If you are not moving forward you would know of potential weaknesses that you might wish changing or addressing in the future.

If something about you that is important or impressive was somehow overlooked or not acknowledged by the interviewer ask a question designed to direct the conversation in the direction. Such as "I noticed in the job posting you mentioned experience in managing remote employees. Did you notice that in my current job I manage a remote field staff of 28 people and have done so for 10 years? During that time we hit almost every goal and exceeded all expectations." This gets the information out there and can help establish you as the premier applicant or candidate.

You should use this portion of the interview to show a passion for the position and the company. Share a few ideas or ask probing questions that highlight your interest in the job. Show your excitement so the interviewer gets the feeling that this is more than a paycheck for you. Don't go overboard but make sure the interviewer sees your excitement and passion.

Ending the Interview

Eventually all good things must come to an end.

When all the questions have been asked and the interviewer is confident that they have all the information they need at that point in time, they will signal the end of the interview.

Regardless of how the interview had gone and whether you feel you did a good job or a poor one, than the interviewer with a smile and remain positive. Keep in mind that it is not your opinion that matters now but the opinion of the interviewer that counts. Don't make any excuses or apologize for doing poorly even if you feel that way. Such statements can only reflect negatively upon you and possible raise doubt in the mind of the interviewer.

If it feels right you can inquire as to what the next step in the process might be and when those decisions are likely to be made. If the interviewer wishes to let you in on that information he or she will do so. If not, they will just tell you that someone will be in touch with you. Don't push then about this. Just accept the answer they give you and move on.

Thank the interviewer for taking the time out of their day to talk to you and tell them you enjoyed the experience even if it was comparable to hell on earth. You want to appear calm and confident as you end the interview just as you did when you walked in. Keep your head up, keep eye contact and thank the interviewer again.

Then leave the office, thank the secretary or receptionist or whoever else is there and leave the building. Keep up the confident exterior and smile all the way until you're out of the building. Sometimes there are cameras you know and who knows who might be watching.

If a sound a bit paranoid please excuse me but I always believed that the little things make all the difference in the words and if something is possible, act like it is and you will rarely be disappointed!

Now you can relax and drive home or out to lunch or wherever you're going and start the next part of the process. Oh, I'm sorry. Did you think you were done now that the interview is over? Well some people might be done.

But you're not. Not by a long shot.

After the Interview

This can be the most frustrating part of the process as you have completed the interview and now often have no idea whether you will be given the job, asked for a second interview or eliminated from the process for whatever reason. It's not an easy time but there are a few things we can do to make use of our time and prepare us for what might come ahead for us.

The following are a few things everyone should do after any interview. Even when you are told that you are no longer being considered there are benefits to doing each one of these items. After all, no one knows if this same company might have another opening in the near future and you want to be ready to take advantage of it!

Do a Self-Critique or Evaluation

They say hindsight is always 20/20 and by that they mean that after something happens it is easy to see what went right and what went wrong.

This applies to interviews as well. Because of this it is important that we take a few moments right after the interview to think about how things went.

As you do this it is important that you are completely honest with yourself. It will not do you much good if you tell yourself you did great when in fact you didn't. No one other than yourself has to hear your thoughts or read your notes. This is strictly for you and you are the one that benefits from the process.

Ask yourself how the interview went overall. Were you calm or nervous? Was the interviewer impressed and positive or did they seem bored or eager to end things early? Did you have good and impressive answers to every question or were there a couple that stumped you or that you didn't have good answers? Did you fall short on anything such as education or specific experience? What do you think the interviewers liked and didn't like about you? What comments did the interviewer make about certain things?

All of this is important because you can use all of this as feedback that will help you do better in a second interview or for the interview for the next job you applied for. This way you learn from your recent interview so you can be more impressive and effective next time.

But be honest with yourself and do this right after the interview. Do not wait a day or a week as some details and information are forgotten over time.

Do it while you remember every little detail. Because sometimes it is the little things that can make the biggest difference.

Make Notes About the Interview

As you are doing your self-evaluation or critique, think about what you have learned and write down notes that will help you remember certain things about the interview. Include the questions you either couldn't answer or didn't answer well enough. Write down the high and low points and what the interviewer seemed to like or dislike.

Don't think you will always remember these things because you won't. They will get blurred over time and you need to remember them just like they happened yesterday. Then once you are done, do something with your notes. Correct the little things that you think went wrong. Research those tough questions and come up with better or more effective answers. In other words, turn what are your current interview weaknesses into strengths.

This is very important as it will help you understand what you need to do moving forward. If moving forward means you are getting a second interview, you can use the information in your notes to determine your approach and focus from the last interview.

Often you can tell from the questions and the attitude of the interviewer what the company really is looking for or what is more important in the eyes of the company.

Knowing this from the first interview will help you change answers a bit and give them more of what they are looking for. Changing your answers a bit to make them more targeted to what the company wants is a very effective way of making yourself look better and a better match to the position and the company.

If moving forward is an interview for another job in the near future, your notes can help you better prepare and identify weaknesses that need a bit of work. Everyone has them so don't try and fool yourself into thinking you don't. You do have weaknesses and understanding them will help you eliminate them for the next interview.

Send a Follow-Up thankyou Note

Here is something a lot of applicant don't do and I am not sure why. They are either lazy or just don't think of doing this but it can be one of the smartest things you can do after an interview and it only takes a few minutes to do.

Think about the interviewer for a moment. Chances are they interviewed several other candidates around the same time they interviewed you. Whenever that happens little details are lost and the candidates seem to blur together a bit.

So unless you made a super impression that just could not be forgotten you run the risk of the interviewer forgetting which candidate you were. But if you send them a follow-up thank you note thanking them for spending time with you, that can help refresh their memory and bring you and your interview back into focus.

You can also add little details such as how excited you are about the position and maybe a detail or two about relevant experience and education so they remember exactly who you are. If it accomplishes nothing else, writing the letter shows that you are really interested about the position and that this was not just one of 20 interviews you went on this week. Showing that you have passion and interest is never a bad thing.

Prepare for the Next Round Should it Come!

The one thing everyone hopes comes after a first interview is the coveted second interview. This is where the pool of applicants shrinks even further and if you make it to this level, there is definitely interest in you.

As we already recommended, you hopefully have some notes and ideas about how the first interview went. This information can be critical in helping you prepare for the second interview.

We will be discussing second and third interviews shortly but for now, let's just say that whatever the first interviewer seemed to focus on should give you a pretty good idea of what they feel is the most important aspects of the job and who they are going to pick to get that job.

Go back and think about what the interviewer said as he described the company and the particular position you are interviewing for. What did they seem to stress about the position and the company? What seemed most important throughout the interview? What did they spend the most time on or ask the most questions about? All of these little bits of information can help you give them more of what they want in the next interview.

Don't sit back and just wait for the next interview. Use that first interview as a building block to help you do even better in the second interview. Doing so will give you a huge advantage over the other applicants who just patted themselves on the back for making it to round two. Don't be one of those applicants. You can pat yourself on the back for making it through but then sit down and use round one to prepare for round two.

Learn from All of Your Interviews

Every interview is a learning experience.

Whether it is just being exposed and getting comfortable with the different styles of interviews or just finding out what you were good and not so good in every interview will help you with the next one.

But they will only help you if you let them. Take the time to go back over them. Dissect them and pick them apart. Make a list of good points and not so good points. Then sit down and figure out what you might have done differently or done better.

Acknowledge your performance and take responsibility for it. Do not blame the interviewer or say that they were unfair or didn't know what they were doing. Even though this might be true, it still doesn't help you prepare for next time if you make excuses for this time. When we accept responsibility we learn from our experiences and we get better and become more productive and effective.

Whenever we blame everyone else, we don't change anything. And when nothing is changed, nothing changes.

Remember that after your next interview.

Additional Interviews

Everyone loves getting the call or the e-mail telling you that they want you back for a second or third interview. It is a sign of success and a confirmation that you performed well in the first interview. After all, only a small percentage of applicants that had that first interview are going to be called back for a second. So you are now in an Elite class of applicants so it is time to step up your game for round two.

In this chapter we are going to go over second and third interviews and what might be different about them. You might be faced with a different interviewer (you probably will) and maybe the style of interview might change as well. But probably the biggest difference is going to be the absence of weak applicants that make you look better by comparison.

Once you get into second or third interviews you are competing against the best of the group. So what was good enough to get you through to round two probably isn't going to be good enough to get you the job.

But don't worry because the first interview was the toughest one. Knowing what you learned from the first interview will give you a heads up about future interviews. And we are going to capitalize on that right now.

Second Interviews

As we have stated, second interviews given to a selected number of applicants, sometimes just one or two, so that more information can be provided to help either confirm a decision that has already been made or to enable a final decision between candidates. Although the interview is likely to be similar to the first interview, there are a few subtle differences.

First, you are going to have to "sell yourself" to the interviewer more because the competition is much higher in later rounds of interviews. You need to carefully craft your answers and approach to get the maximum benefit. You want to pull out all the stops as far as self-promotion is concerned.

Second, be ready for more specific questions regarding your skills and experience. Be prepared to provide specific and relevant examples of how your education and experience ties in closely to the job you are interviewing for. You not only need to connect the dots you have to explain the picture those dots have created.

Third, be prepared for an inexperienced interviewer. This can be a good thing for you because second interviews are sometimes conducted by managers who will be in charge of the applicants. These managers are not trained interviewers so you are likely to get more real-world questions and examples than standard interview questions. If you have a lot of skills and experience second interviews usually go much easier.

Fourth, beware of the "think outside the box" types of questions that sometimes show up in latter stages of interviews. These questions are designed to have you think outside of normal parameters and they can get you into trouble. Always keep your thoughts and ideas within acceptable boundaries and never mention or infer illegal or unethical behavior even if you really would consider using it.

Fifth, play up your interpersonal skills and show them that not only would you be a great fit skill-wise but also personality wise as well. How people get along with each other in the workplace is one of the most important factors when it comes to teamwork and overall productivity. Show them that you can do the job and fit in at the same time and you just might walk out with an offer!

Sixth, speaking of offers, during second interviews the subject of salary and benefits might come up.

Be careful not to sell yourself too short or price yourself out of the market with demands that are too high. Instead, try and get them to give you a salary range for the position first and go from there. The same with benefits. Ask them what they offer and go from there. If salary does not come up you can ask about it in a generalized fashion at the second interview.

Seventh, it is a good idea for the applicant to ask at least a few questions as well in advanced interviews. Ask questions about job responsibilities, share your thoughts and ideas for the position and ask how they think you might make the position more productive. Show a passion for the job and all that it entails.

Eighth, throughout the entire interview, make sure you articulate your message clearly and strongly. Show a passion for the job and make sure that you get your entire message across to the interviewer. This is possibly your last opportunity to get your full message across so make sure you take advantage of it.

Ninth, and we save the most important for last, make sure that you have a plan going into the interview. Leave nothing to chance and make sure you know what you want to say and how you want to say it.

Interviewers at this level are very willing to hear specifics you have to offer as long as they are relevant to the position. Have a plan, follow that plan to the letter, and get your message across!

As far as after the interview is concerned, follow the same practices that you followed after the first interview. Evaluate your performance, make notes as to what went right or wrong and send the follow-up letter or e-mail. Remember you are not done with the process so keep up the efforts and make sure everyone knows you are still interested and excited about the position.

Third Interviews and Beyond

While most jobs will require just one or two interviews, some higher level position might require three or more interviews. The framework for these interviews will pretty much follow the theme of the second interviews only with different people conducting them. In some cases at least one of the interviews might be a panel or group interview where you interview with several people at one. Or, you might be called in to interview with several people one after another until you have met with everyone.

Generally as the interviews progress the questions will get more specific and more detailed. You will be asked to demonstrate knowledge and decision making capabilities as well as offering insight into the position and you vision for it.

For positions higher up in the company they might ask you more questions about the industry itself and where you see the company going within that industry.

The best thing about these interviews is that you have already demonstrated the skills education and experience for the position. At this point you might be the only candidate left or one of two. These interviews are generally just to get exposure to more people and to have those people "sign off" on bringing you on-board.

You will probably find these interviews less confrontational or stressful as both you and the company have already established a certain comfort level with each other. But this can be dangerous as well. Comfort and familiarity often results in people letting down their guard and possibly saying things they shouldn't. Always be on guard and do not risk anything by saying something you will regret later.

Be calm and professional and answer all questions openly and honestly while watching what you say and how you say it. If you play your cards right and prove to be a good fit both skills-wise and personality-wise you should walk away with a firm offer and hopefully, the job.

Exiting the Process

Eventually there will come a time when the process is finished. Hopefully you were the one picked for the position, the offer was great, and now you are in a better job which is what your goal was all along. But maybe things didn't work out the way you had hoped for some reason and the position went to someone else. Either way, the process has ended and now it is time to wrap things up and move on.

Here are a few things you can do to make sure you get the most from the experience and possibly improve your chances for next time if things didn't work out well this time. If that is the case please don't get discouraged! It is rare for someone to get an offer for every job they apply for. There is just too much competition these days. Instead, try and learn as much as you can from your experience so that you become better and stronger because of it.

Learning from the Process

The best thing we can do when the process is completed is to look back and learn as much from the experience as we can.

We should do this whether we received a job offer or not. Acknowledging success allows us to identify behaviors that worked well and use them again in the future. Acknowledging failures allows us to identify things we didn't do very well and improve those weaknesses.

It is easy to learn when things go wrong because our disappointment often leads into contemplation about what happened and we learn from that process. But when things go right we often don't delve into things much deeper because we got the desired result. But even when things go right we can still learn from the experience so we should still go through the process.

The whole idea is to use our experiences to become better, stronger and more prepared for next time. This applies not only to interviews but most all other parts of life as well. Experience something, learn from the experience and move on better and stronger for it.

Re-Evaluating Your Approach

Sometimes we move ahead in a direction that looking back we realize wasn't the right choice. This doesn't mean we made an error or mistake, we just chose the wrong approach to something with all the best intentions. It's not like we intended to fail when we started out, it just worked out that way.

But when things don't work out it is important to understand why. Maybe our approach was wrong and we can determine that by evaluating what happened. If it is shown the approach was wrong, discover why it was wrong so you don't make the same choices next time. This isn't about being right or wrong it is about getting the right results the next time.

Remember if we continue to do the same things and follow the same paths, we are usually going to wind up at the same destination. So discover where you went wrong, make the required changes and get closer to your intended destination next time or the time after that.

Getting Professional Help

Sometimes we go through something and give it our best but come up short. We make adjustments and get a bit further or better next time but still come up short. In times like these you might decide that you can save time, and perhaps some money as well, by getting some professional assistance.

There are personal coaches who can help you with your presentation skills and help you with your confidence. There are people who specialize in resume design and will create a professional resume and cover letters for you if you have trouble doing that yourself.

There are people who can give you mock interviews so you can make changes to your approach and performance before actually going out on interviews. There are courses you can take on public speaking as well.

Whether you need any of these resources is up to you. There is no hard and fast rule and the ultimate decision is based on personal preference. If I were to offer any opinion it might be that if you have gone on 3 or more interviews and have not been chosen for an advanced interview or offered a job, perhaps you might consult with someone to get an idea why.

If you haven't gone on any interviews you really don't know whether you need this assistance or not. There is a first time for everything and maybe you should get one or two interviews under your belt and see how you do. Then, if you feel you need some outside help, go out and get it.

Outside or professional help usually does not come cheap. But if it will save you time and help you get your career moving ahead faster and easier it might be worthwhile to you. If you lack a specific skill, such as the ability to write well, then this might suggest hiring someone to help you out in that area might be helpful.

This entire process is not difficult but it does require certain skills and attributes. Most, if not all, can easily be learned but that will take time. That is why we suggested you start the learning process early before you need to go on an important interview. But if you don't have the time and an opportunity is staring you in the face, getting some outside help just might be what you need to respond quickly to an opportunity that might not be there tomorrow.

Common sources for professional help with interviews or resumes can usually be found in the local Yellow pages or via an internet search for local groups or organizations. Your local community colleges or business associations sometimes are great sources as well.

Adult education and sometimes your local department of labor or unemployment office have job searching and interview classes that can help build your confidence and performance. Some of these resources might be free while others might have a modest fee. The first place I would check is your local unemployment office as they usually have a listing of the resources available to local residents.

Of course there are also books like this one and videos for people who don't want scheduled courses or people who can't attend a structured class. Books are free at the library and there are sure to be a wealth of books on this subject there for free.

If you feel you need the help, by all means get it. Because some people need it to get where they want to be achieve some of the goals they have set for themselves. If you need the help, get it and don't be ashamed of it either. It takes a lot of courage to admit you need help so take pride in the fact that you are strong enough to seek out help.

Don't let personal pride stand in the way of you getting the help you need to succeed.

Starting All Over

Chances are most of us are going to be starting all over again either now or the next time we want to make a change in our careers. There is nothing wrong in starting over. It is a part of life. But learning is also a part of life and every time we start over we start out a little bit smarter and a little bit more aware.

I don't think that not getting a job offer means that you failed. If you went through the interview process and learned something that made you a better applicant and a better person at the same time, you really cannot call that failure. I call it learning.

I think we need to measure success and failure in terms of how an experience helped make us stronger or better in life. If we go on 3 interviews and gain experience that helps us get a job out of interview #4, who is to say that we failed the first three times? Most people experience a series of failures before they become successful. It's just how life works.

Yeah, I know that means very little to the person who has come up short time and time again. But if we learn something each time that is what is important. It is when we don't learn and make the same mistakes over and over and over again that the word failure has some mean for us.

Learn from your past, make changes as you move forward and improve your knowledge and performance. Eventually you will succeed and that success will be that much sweeter because you know you worked hard for it. Very little in life is handed to us and most people are not successful the first time out. But when you are finally successful you will be able to look back and see how your past failures made you better and stronger.

But as long as there are goals to achieve and steps to take, there will be failure. Success isn't as much about success as it is about our past failures. We all have them. It is just what we do with them that separates the successful from the rest of the pack.

Additional Resources

If you would like some more resources on Career Growth or Resume Preparation, please check out our other titles:

Career Hacks!

Resume Hacks!

All "Hacks!" Books are available wherever you purchased this title!